LIFE WITH THE SMITHTON STREET GANG

J.J. Ehrhardt

PublishAmerica
Baltimore

First printing

PublishAmerica has allowed this work to remain exactly as the author intended, verbatim, without editorial input.

Hardcover 978-1-4560-0052-3
Softcover 978-1-4560-0053-0
PUBLISHED BY PUBLISHAMERICA, LLLP
www.publishamerica.com
Baltimore

Printed in the United States of America

Dedicated to: Paul "Juice" Trunick

In Loving Memory of my Parents:

Ruth Dorothy "Ehrhardt" Lodge,
James Joseph Ehrhardt Sr.

fond memory of: Jimmy 'Pajamas' Long
Frank 'The Animal' Vikkers
and Richard Lee 'Hardhead' Macik

"There is a destiny that keeps us brothers,
None walks his way alone.
All that we send into the lives of others,
Comes back into our own."
A Creed:Edwyn Markham

September 30, 2005

Porjy Retterback, Don Retterback, Jimmy Long, Paul Trunick, Jamie Parker, Jimmy Ehrhardt, Jackie Hunt, Rusty Waxler

Smithton Street Gang Photo

INTRODUCTION

Judging from the passages those of you who were so kind to donate, it was a very special time for you, too. When asked to give me your input, you were kind and did not hesitate to do so, which was very much appreciated.

Many long hours were spent writing the following material. It contains a collection of memories of special times being born, and/or growing up in a unique part of Pittsburgh, PA...Smithton Street. Those of you who lived there, or maybe even spent some time there, know of a somewhat mystical power that made you want to stay and share the fun that evolved there.

If you are reading this, and you spent some time there, I'm sure there are countless memories that run through some of your minds, and perhaps you feel the need to call and reminisce. If this be the case, feel free to do that, because I'm gathering suggestions and material for another book right now!

I thought I had picked the most endearing ones for now, however...or I would spend eternity writing about all of them. I'm writing this as if it is a 300 page book, and truly in my heart, I have every intention of doing so some time, but I thought I couldn't hold my loving family and dear friends in suspense any longer. The material you are about to read is truly nonfictional, but some names have been changed to protect the innocent. So here it goes!

Many of the nicknames in the following material that have been mentioned in Chapter 12A, page 34, were called by John Orman (a.k.a. lump Chapter 27), I will go over with you most of them, and describe them for you.

Ehr, (pronounced ear, I got this nickname from Roy Sears, a black child in high school who could not pronounce my last name. Harpo: I got this nickname from the Gang because of my wild curly hair, and my love of the Marx Brothers. By the Way I am Jim Ehrhardt 5 ft. 11 3/4(when standing) white /blond naturally curly hair throughout childhood,. I did try to straighten it out countless ways and times, you know, Vaseline, peach pomade, bacon grease, (although I had every animal in the neighborhood following me around) mechanics ball bearing grease (not really, although it sounds like it would work) little did I know, it would straighten with age. It's now light brown and straight as an arrow. Blue eyes. Very loud, fond of animals (especially dogs, bears, and skunks) very outgoing, love to socialize.

Was always left-handed before THE FALL (Chapter 32). Now I am right hand dominant. Mustache, drifting right eye (due to lazy eye disease (medical term: amblyopia pronounced—am-blee-OH-pee-uh), defined: Decreased vision in one or both eyes without detectable anatomic damage to the retina or visual pathways. Usually uncorrectable by eyeglasses or contact lenses. (PS: just thought I'd throw that in)

Jackie' Smoke 'Hunt: (my cousin and friend throughout our childhood years): 6 foot rust colored hair, blue eyes. He had one sister named Judy.

Tic, Sausage, Pajamas-Rusty Waxler: my best friend throughout our childhood and teen years.) 5 ft. 9 sandy, brown hair, blue eyes. His older sister was Janet and he had an older brother Butch.

Fond of sports (especially baseball and football) participated in plenty of them throughout his childhood and teen years.

Nut-Porjy Retterback, Rusty's cousin, just as tall as him, sandy brown hair, brown eyes. Most fearless of the gang, had a reputation for being hard core, but to his friends, he was as gentle as a lamb. He loved being with the guys, and we always enjoyed having him around. He had a knack for getting into trouble, although, and it usually found him. He was the oldest boy of seven children, Jackie was the oldest girl, and then came Sissy, Kathy, Donald, Mary Ann, and finally the baby, Kelly. More about Porjy and Rusty later on in the book.

CHAPTER 1.

Tin Can Alley

"One, two, three, tin can Alley" Rusty would call out, and let the can fly. We all would run our separate ways, hiding here and there, under cars, between houses, even seven blocks away, up on a Dairy Queen Roof, (I will explain this one later in the book).

The rules for Tin Can Alley were as follows: you gather a bunch of kids (the Smithton St. gang will suffice, usually it was Porjy and Don Retterback, Rusty, Me,, Paul, Jimmy Long, occasionally my cousin Jackie, Rich Macik, or Tank and Timmy Arlet. Everybody stands around the same manhole cover. You pick one kid to be it (usually me, or any of the other slower kids) and another kid to throw the can (usually Paul, because he was the biggest & it seemed he could throw it for two city blocks). Once the can is thrown, the kids scatter and hide. The person who is it, has to run, retrieve the can, set it back on the manhole cover, and locate each and every other kid.

Once he sees somebody hiding (i.e.: Rusty on Mrs. Keenan's roof), he would go back to base (manhole) grab the can, smack it on the manhole three times and say: one, two, three on Rusty hiding on Mrs. Keenan's roof and so on until every kid is found. The first player caught is usually ' it.' the next round.

There is, however, a rule that permits a player (usually Paul) to "release" the other players by sneaking into base, grabbing the can, smacking it on the manhole, and yelling at the top of his lungs "1-2-3 Tin Can Alley," throwing the can (usually two city blocks), and the player who is it, (usually me), has to track everybody down again. One time, one of our slow minded friends, Jimmy Lang, climbed up on a Dairy Queen roof seven blocks away. Clearly out of bounds. We never did find him, but he didn't care, he probably fell asleep there and stayed the whole night, only to get himself in trouble with his foster mother, Ruth Waxler. He was always in trouble with her, maybe that's because he was so different.

How do you decide who to marry?

You got to find somebody who likes the same stuff. Like, if you like sports, she should like it that you like sports, and she should keep the pretzels, chips and dip coming.—Alan, age 10

Do not walk ahead of me, I may not follow. Do not walk behind me, I may not lead. Do not walk beside me either. Just pretty much leave me the hell alone. ~Unknown

CHAPTER 1B.

Linda "Sparkle Plenty" Ehrhardt

A poem from Florence Sherrill Ferrell
For my sister, Brothers and Sisters
From where love came, we cannot see:
Perhaps, within us, born and bred,
Or taught to us at parent's knee,
Or instilled by God in heart and head.
Perhaps it sprang from some kind deed,
which, long forgotten, yet has grown
to dazzling heights from one small seed
In the fertile soil of distress sown.
The pettiness of separate view;
Differences bow before a love
And friendship that is blood-bound, too.
May the bond between us stronger grow,
May I prove the fondness I confess,
Which my hand's service cannot show'
Nor my simple words ever express.

More beautiful words were never penned.
    One of the earliest recollections of my older sister Linda
(my father started calling her Sparkle Plenty at an early age, I

took over later in life, when he passed) entails my mother getting my cousin Jackie and I each a toy car (they were about three quarter the size of a crackerjack box), and if my memory serves me right, they were Lincoln Continental convertibles. We were about seven years old at the time, and my mother, knowing that I like the color blue, gave me the blue one & Jackie the green one.

Jackie wanted the blue one, and tried his early psychology course on me, "big baby, has to have his own way, and get the blue car." Jackie got the blue one alright, I wailed it at him (I think he still has the mark in his cheek).

Well...that started World War III, fisticuff heaven. Although, Jackie always won the battles, because I started crying first. Jackie was taught never to cry, (ask him, he will tell you the story) I'll bet you're wondering where Linda fits in, she heard the screaming and crying, and came running to see what was the matter.

When she found out why I was crying, she immediately asked my mother where she bought the cars.

When my mother told her they came from Pernatovski's five & dime, Linda immediately went there and bought Jackie and I another green & blue car out of her allowance money. (She probably won't remember that, but I will never forget)

She stood by me through many occasions as I with her. There was the time she had ringworm, and had to have her head shaved, I would not let anybody tease her, and when they did, I comforted her. There was the time she was being punished for not washing dishes correctly, my dad made her go everywhere with a pot tied around her neck. I knew it would be embarrassing for her, so I grabbed a rubber ball & told everyone it was a game we were playing.

She & Linda Stigler were really a team, they were really goofy together. I can remember them playing phone gags. One of them would call Stotlers pharmacy and ask Ray Stotler "do you have Prince Albert (a certain pipe tobacco) in a can?" Stotler would smile & play along, hearing it a thousand times before, "yes, I have Prince Albert in a can." Lynn & Stigler would say, "would you please, let him out!"

There was the time, Stigler called one of her most vain male classmates & talked very sexy to him, got real confidential with him, told him she could fulfill some of his wildest fantasies, told him she went by the name Tiger. Had him going long and strong, would not let up. But suddenly, she said her father was coming, she had to hang up, gave him a phone number, told him to call it and ask for Tiger in 15 minutes. Yes, the girls were really crucial that day, the number they gave him, was the number for the Pittsburgh Zoo!!!

The girls would watch Chiller Theater with Us (See Chapter 3) when the movies were over, and they woke me up, Sparkle would say, "I'm in the mood for a salad & some homemade potato chips!" Stigler would go to the refrigerator, pullout all the salad stuff, while Sparkle would pull out the deep fryer & potatoes. At two o'clock in the morning, we would feast. Best damn salad & potato chips I've had to this day. In her prime, Sparkle had an array of beau's. As a matter of fact, she had a boyfriend for every letter in the alphabet except for "X." She even had a Quako, a Vick, a Wes, a Yorko (short for Yurkovich), and a Zeke.

She had a parakeet, she named Gina. Smartest damn bird I've ever seen. Gina would dance if you sang to her. She would bob her head to the music, & dance all around the kitchen table. Rusty and I used to play checkers at that table, Gina would fly down, pick up the checkers, move them all around, until we swooshed her away. She would just keep doing it until we gave up, and quit playing.

One day, when Jackie and I were home alone playing chess at the kitchen table, I had my back to the window, the window was open, but the expandable screen was in. We let Gina out of the cage, and went in the living room to watch TV. Commercial came on, I went into the kitchen to see what she was up to. There was no sign of her. We looked all around her usual hiding places, no Gina.

I went over to the window, discovered a small opening in the screen, just barely enough for her little body to squeeze through. I was heartbroken; we went outside to call her, thinking that there might be a small chance of catching her, to no avail. Gina was no more, how could I ever tell Sparkle?

She came home from her job at St. John's hospital and I broke the news to her. She went upstairs and cried, I felt so bad, I yelled up the steps, "I will replace her, I promise." The next day, the two of us went downtown to GC Murphy's to get another bird. We came home with "Gina two." Taught her to do some tricks, but it wasn't the same. Life goes on. I learned my lesson about the window.

We had our fair share of arguments too. One afternoon, I was arguing with my mother, we were going back and forth for about half an hour, you know, he said, she said, sort of thing. When all of a sudden, Sparkle cashed her own two cents in, in my mother's favor.

Disgusted & defeated, I stopped her dead in her tracks by yelling out, "you stay out of this, I can lose this battle all by myself!

She later writes:
"Smithton Street. Just the two words bring a wave of nostalgia so strong that it nearly knocks me off my feet!

I'm a full-grown adult, a senior citizen, for Goodness Sake, but just mention Smithton Street and I'm ten again with my little brother, "My Jimmy" by my side. There was nothing or no one at all, I loved more at that time of my life and for long time after. He is a part of my heart like no other. I teased him, defended him, protected him and he was "My Jimmy"!

And now for my "Smithton Street" memories. There are, of course, way too many to write here, I'm saving a lot for my own book! But I've written a few of my very favorite ones.

First and Foremost, would of course be all of our friends, and there were plenty. Many from the same families. There was Sis, Jackie, Porjy and Don, Paul, and more siblings, Janny and Rusty, Sandra and Marlene, Jimmy Long, Don and Billy, and Don Parker, and our cousins Jack and Judy. The list is long and if I didn't write down all the names, it is only because I am a bit older and more forgetful!

We loved our neighborhood. We played ball, Jimmy was on the Little League team and I was part of the team. I was the scorekeeper for some time. The evenings were long and the best part of the day. (Except for the summertime).We all played games like: Kick the can, King of the Hill, Red Rover, Simon says, Monster, Hide and Go Seek, and many, many more. The winters were absolutely fantastic.

We would sled ride down Smithton, it was just enough of a hill to get a good ride, yet the traffic was very light, so we were all pretty safe.

Then, another favorite was our Saturday nights with Chilly Billy Car dilly and "Chiller Theatre". Paul, Jimmy and I were regulars.

There were always two movies. We all made it through the first movie, but Jimmy was sound asleep in the middle of the second. We would try to send him up to bed, but he would insist he was only "resting his eyes." We would physically send him on his way, but there he would be, standing on the steps to the upstairs, leaning against the wall, sound asleep. But, before he went to sleep, I usually would cook us something to snack on. And, of course, it couldn't be anything normal. It would be fried chicken, French fries or homemade potato chips. My best friend, Linda, would sometimes be a part of our Saturday night routine, but she preferred salad, and she only liked the way that I made it, so I would make that for her.

I was always being punished, for one reason or another, forgetting to put the dishes away. Not scrubbing the pots or dishes well enough, (I did them from the time I was five years old). I would be grounded or have some other kind of different penalty.

One time, my dad made me where a small saucepot, with a handle around my neck on a string, I was told to wear that the whole day. I was 10 years old and Jimmy was five. It was a Saturday, and on that day, I usually went to the store for my mother. My dad said I had to wear the pot to the store. I was so embarrassed; I didn't know what to do. Jimmy came up with a bright idea that we were playing a game.

He said he would wad up paper balls, and try to throw them into the pot while I was swinging it back and forth. Well, he really saved me from that total embarrassment.

We had so many happy times. Sleepovers and going swimming at Riverview Park. Neighborhood picnics, and sitting out on the steps in nice weather. Everyone helped each other and all helped the children. Smithton Street was definitely a neighborhood from "days long by." I wish I was still in touch with my very dear friends from that time. I miss them very much. Jackie and Sissy, especially. Their home was a second home for me. I loved it there.

I guess that is why we have our memories. Our "pictures of the past."

How do you decide who to marry?

No person really decides before they grow up whom they're going to marry. God decides it all, way before, and you get to see later who you're stuck with.—Kristen, age 10

The journey of a thousand miles begins with a broken fan belt and leaky tire—unknown

CHAPTER 2.

Jimmy Long

Jimmy Long (God rest his soul) was just weird Jimmy Long, if you search the English-language looking for words to describe him, you would probably get lost in there. People have had a hard time describing him, but I will try.

He was tall & lanky, Long dark brown hair, always playing with it, he had a bald spot he obtained at age 6 just above his forehead, he kept constantly trying to cover it with the rest of his hair, constant motion. He was very intelligent, in his own sort of way. He could recite the stats of every baseball player in the league by heart, but he had trouble remembering his middle name.

He made up a baseball game with baseball cards sprawled out over his living room floor, he pretended that they were on a baseball field, and he would have the prospective players at each one of their positions. He used a little aluminum foil ball, and pretended to pitch it to his baseball card "batter". He actually had a windup motion for his baseball card "pitcher" it was a sight to see, he used little Chiclets for bases.

He was born in 1949 and taken in by Al & Ruth Waxler, Rusty's Aunt and uncle. When he was eight years old, his real mother and father abused him by scalding him with hot rice when he was quite young, and he lived in different Foster homes ever since.

I talked about him so much to Maggie, she felt as if she knew him. And then one day, as we were driving down Brighton Road. We passed the Cemetery Road, and Maggie said to me, (never meeting or seeing the man before,) "there's Jimmy Long" I asked her where, she pointed him out to me, and sure enough, it was him coming down the road!

I asked him what he's been doing all these years, and he said he had just gotten out of prison. I wasn't shocked, what I was shocked about, was the reason, he said he did a bum rap for Child molestation! Child molestation, our Jimmy Long, Will wonders ever cease.

WHAT IS THE RIGHT AGE TO GET MARRIED?
No age is good to get married. You got to be stupid to get married.—Freddie, age 6

It's always darkest before dawn. So if you're going to steal your neighbors' newspaper, that's the best time to do it.—unknown

21

CHAPTER 3.

Paul "Juice" Trunick

Paul Trunick would stay the furthest from base of our Tin Can Alley mainly because he was the fastest. It might be because he had size 22 feet or because he was six-foot four inches at age twelve (well it seemed like it anyway). He had a quick draw temper that was surpassed only by his dog Teddy, who was so mean; he had hair on his tongue! I swear the dog could breathe fire. His mother was set in her ways also, many a time we asked her for different things, only to be turned down. She has mellowed out over the years, and now to this day, she is one of the sweetest people.

Paul, Sparkle, and I used to watch Chilly Billy on Chiller Theater together religiously. Every Saturday night 11:30 P.m. right after the News at my House, of course. Sparkle would make popcorn, and pink lemonade.

They aired two movies; I would always fall asleep before the first was over. Paul, and her would end up watching them both, they would always wake me after the movies, to fill me in on what happened. She would end up making us homemade French fried potato chips in the fryer (cholesterol heaven) and more pink lemonade.

One night, Paul gathered enough nerve to ask his mother if I could stay at his house to watch Chiller Theater, with her powerful NO!, she loosened the plaster on the walls, and melted Paul's eyebrows, he was standing right in front of her. He turned to tell me he was sorry, but I was already home.

Paul's Alley was another thing. It ran the depth of the house (about 30 feet), and it was between the two houses of 1067 and 1069 Smithton, 1069 has been torn down since. There were no lights to help you see. IT WAS PITCH FREAKIN' BLACK! There was the doorway from hell halfway up the Alley; we swear it had the bogeyman waiting to grab you if you weren't quick enough. We would take a running start at the front of the house, and run up that Alley as fast as possible.

If you weren't fast enough, the man in the doorway from hell would get you. The reason Paul was so fast, was because he had to run past the doorway from hell every night.

One night while I was running up the Alley, I ran smack dab into the railing. Needless to say, I went down. Writhing with Pain, I laid there motionless, hoping the man in the doorway from hell wouldn't get me.

I must have laid there for what seemed like hours, before I gathered enough courage to get up and run, I'm here to say, that was a close one.

Paul and I had this crazy idea one afternoon, after watching a cowboy and Indian movie, to become blood Brothers! (How's this one sound, Dr. Rossman?) We went to my mother's kitchen drawer, and picked out a single sharp knife (still listening Dr. Rossman?) Then we proceeded to go outside.

Why it had to be done outside is beyond me. We went across the street of Frank Inskipt's house and proceeded as planned.

Starting with Paul, he cut himself across the right palm, (very deeply, I might add), he then handed the knife to me. I countered, by doing the same thing. Needless to say, we had blood squirting everywhere, without saying a word; we clasped each others right hands, and hugged. After a long while, he turned to me and said, "I love you brother," I said the same. We have been calling each other "brother" ever since.

WHAT IS THE RIGHT AGE TO GET MARRIED?

Twenty-four is the best age because you know the person forever by then.—Camille, age 10

Don't be irreplaceable. If you can be replaced, you can't be promoted.—unknown

CHAPTER 4.

Smithton St. Layout

My daughter called, and asked if I can go into detail about the old neighborhood houses, so here goes. Starting up a small grade on Smithton, to your right, you have the Camino Twins grandfather's house.

Continuing up the hill, Inglis Street will be on your right, home of the Camino Twins, Dan & Don, their older brother Fred, and their father, Al, (one of the finest carpenters on the North Side of Pittsburgh).

At the top of Inglis on your left, was Mr. Hricik, who used to pee off his porch every Sunday when the ladies were coming home from church. We fixed him though; we set a flaming bag of doggy poop on his porch, rang his bell, and ran like hell. He came out to find a fire, stomping like crazy in his stocking feet. We just stood down in the street and laughed our heads off. Continuing on Inglis Street, last, but not least, was Macik's on the left.

Continuing on Smithton, was Nicky Capo's house on the right (Nicky, Chuck's Buddy, was too old for us) there was Tripoli's, With Wild Bill & Tokyo YoYo (our name for Mrs.

Tripoli)', Paul's house (1069, no longer there), Jimmy Long's (1067), my House (1065), the Keenan's (1061, who were Timmy and Tank Arlet's grandparents). Frank & Barb Inskipt at 1059, Jackie Hunt at 1057. 1055 belonged to the Waxler's (Rusty's parents.). Next to them, lived the Retterback's, all seven of them at 1051 living on the second floor, while Gramps (Porjy and Donald's grandfather), lived below. The Furman's, (Jackie's grandparents) at 1049, up next you had the Benton's (Jackie's aunt and uncle) at 1047, we will stop at wild Orman's house at 1045 (see Chapter 27)

HOW CAN A STRANGER TELL IF TWO PEOPLE ARE MARRIED

You might have to guess, based on whether they seem to be screaming at the same kids.—Dante, age 8

Always remember that you're unique. Just like everyone else.—unknown

CHAPTER 5.

Monster Club & Show

We were infatuated with monsters, we had a monster club. Paul was president (naturally) I was Treasurer; Rusty was vice president, & Secretary.

As Treasurer, I got to carry the cash box, I remember it well, it was a little pirate treasure box with a tiny lock, and an even tinier key. It was my job to collect money every week. The dues were five cents a week, and I remember gathering a total of 40¢ before we stopped doing it. The dues went to buying Monster Magazine; we didn't even gather enough money to buy it. The Magazine sold for 50¢

One time, we decided to put on a monster show in our empty downstairs apartment. It was a small 12 x 15 room, with a seating capacity of six, two kids showed up, we had to beg a third one, Georgie Richert, to come (he got in free, of course). Paul was Frankenstein (naturally). I'll never forget, Don played a young boy who discovers Frankenstein. The way we rehearsed it was Don was to say, "look at the big man" Paul, as Frankenstein, was to pick him up and physically throw him on a staged empty cot. So he would land safely.

After Don said his famous line, Paul picked him up over his head, and let him fly. He missed his mark however, and hit the floor with a huge THUD! which shook the house? Don put a scare in all of us that day, because he laid there motionless, until our little act was over, Georgie Richert pissed his pants. Don was fine however, a little bruised, but fine. I played Count Dracula, using my mothers black lace stole as a cape. Frankenstein killed me off too, only much gentler.

One of us, had the brainy idea to substitute ketchup for real blood. I had it all over me, up my nose, in my ears, all over my mothers stole. I wasn't fooling anybody, it looked like ketchup, and smelled like ketchup. One of our young audience members yelled out, "Ooo yuck, I'll bet his mother is gonna beat him for getting ketchup all over himself." The play grossed us 50¢, enough to buy an issue Of Monster Magazine!

WHAT DO YOU THINK YOUR MOM AND DAD HAVE IN COMMON?

Neither one want any more kids.—Lana, age 8

Never test the depth of water with both feet—unknown

CHAPTER 6.

Chuck" Legs" Wooster

Chuck got his nickname from Huntzy Furman because he was tall, lanky, and all legs. Although my mother called him Charlie, I took over calling him that when she passed. It's funny how things turn around, I call him Charlie, he likes to be called Chuck, he calls his only son Charlie, and his son likes to be called Chuck (does that confuse the hell out of you, or what)

We played monsters, monsters was invented and created by Chuck Wooster. Chuck was our idol, he was seven years older than me, and it was awesome when we could get him to play monsters with us, which was rarely, he was too busy with girls, and all that mushy stuff.

Chuck was THE werewolf, he played the part, he had the growl down pat. Nobody, not even Paul Trunick (who later took over Chuck's job as head monster) could growl like that. Monster playing area was one city block, believe it or not, including the Cemetery, which ran the whole length of all our houses. We actually had a Cemetery for our backyard!

The rules for monsters were: everybody started at base (manhole cover) Chuck and all. He made us promise to close our eyes, and count to 100 by twos. We always cheated, but it didn't matter to him, he would disappear before we got to 20. Paul and he (hence the nickname "legs") were the two fastest people in the world, I swear. Chuck also made us promise to walk alone, no buddy system, so we obliged.

Once you see him, (which we never did) you were to scream out at the top of your lungs, "WEREWOLF IN HUNT'S BACK YARD or WEREWOLF BEHIND WAXLER'S PINE TREE" Chuck was supposed to turn himself in (which he never did). But, before he caught you, he would growl his famous growl first, which you heard, but never knew where it was coming from. (It would scare the shit out of you).

He would sneak up on you, you would never, ever hear him coming, grab you, (you would shit some more), and take you to Gramp's wall, lay you on the wall, stick an old piece of pipe in the ground beside your head and say, "when you can pull that pipe out of the ground with your nose, you are free to go. Needless to say, we stayed there until our mothers called us in.

He now writes:

"The time of my life when I lived on Smithton Street was one of the best times of my life. From when I was 10 years old to about 12 I lived with the Ehrhardt's. Ruth, my other mother, and Jim who had taken the place of my father.

They took me and mother in when my mother and Dad got divorced, and really took care of us. I do not know what would have happened to Mom and me if they hadn't. Linda and Jimmy were the brother and sister I never had.

Christmas time was especially great because Jim would always put up the best tree you ever saw with a platform of a village that was spectacular. Everybody loved baseball and we used to play "rundown" with all the kids, Jimmy, Rusty, Porjy, Paul, and many more. I was the oldest and was King of the Mountain, at least until Lump(see Chapter 27) would come along and scare us all away.

I remember playing in the cemetery for hours, whether it was Army or just going to the dump, the cemetery was a very friendly place for all of us. I remember Porjy cutting his foot at the dump and carrying him back home.Hey, we were all friends and would do anything for each other.

Smithton Street is where I met my best friend for over 50 years, Nicky Capo. Smithton Street was a place for the first time in my early life that I was really happy. It was a place that I felt a part of a bigger family...all my friends.

One of my favorite memories was playing Werewolf and chasing everyone. I particularly remember chasing and scaring to death Paul Trunick. I had never met anyone that loved to have the crap scared out of him like Paul.

You just don't see parents and children play wiffal ball out in the street for hours like we did. Even under the street lights. George Furman, Mr. Hunt, Huntzy, Mr Waxler, good people.

I remember the night the Orman's house caught on fire, and what a spectacular fire it was. Everyone in the neighborhood woke up to the sounds of sirens and fire trucks racing onto Smithton Street.

Later after I left Smithton Street I was reunited with the gang years later when I joined "The Smithton Street Gang" softball team. The team didn't win that many games...but they never lost a fight.

A great memory of even greater people...I was very fortunate to have spent part of my life...living on Smithton Street...a very special place."

WHAT DO MOST PEOPLE DO ON A DATE?

1. Dates are for having a good time! and people should use them to get to know each other. Even boys have something to say if you listen long enough.—Jeanette, age 8

If you think nobody cares if your alive, trying missing a couple of car payments—unknown

CHAPTER 7.

Paul Trunick As the Count.

Paul Trunick took over when Chuck left for the service, he took it one step further, he would roam the neighborhoods and Riverview Park (a beautiful Park beside our neighborhood) dressed in full garb as Count Dracula, in the middle of July! He would wear a long black cape that he borrowed from Rusty. Rusty's mom made it for him for Halloween one year, (she was one hell of a seamstress.), white shirt, black bowtie, black vest, makeup and false teeth. He was a sight to see. He made an awesome Dracula.

One summer night, while he was out running around the neighborhoods as the Count, one of the neighbors called the police. Paul led them on a wild goose chase throughout the neighborhood and up into Riverview Park by way of Break Your Neck Hill. He made it to the top of the hill in a matter of seconds,, with the cops hot on his tail, but they were no match for his speed.

At the top of the hill, he ran smack into a parked car with two lovers in it. He sprawled himself across the windshield to catch his breath. Breathing hard, he stared directly into the faces of the lovers. Needless to say, the two lovers were terrified, the male pulled his pants halfway up, started the car, and took off like a bat out of hell.

Paul caught his breath, and ran again throughout the Park. The cops had no chance of catching him, they gave up the pursuit, however, and he came back and told us of his adventure. All we could do was laugh.

(Speaking about Break Your Neck Hill, it was covered with blueberries, millions of them. We used to stop their before going swimming and gorge ourselves with blueberries. We would get to the pool and have blue mouths, tongues and teeth. People used to look us over and think that we were sick. Back to dress up night.

Rusty and I, were dressed up also that night, he was some sort of ghoul, I was wax man. (I suppose you want to know what wax man was?) The guys talked me into having hot candle wax drip on my face, (I was very naïve in my young age), and they convinced me that if they held the candle high enough, the wax would cool on its way down to my face. Naturally, to fit in, I agreed.

We started out with me laying on the ground looking up at Paul, holding a burning candle about 8 in. above my face. It started dripping down, and I winced all the more with every drop that hit my face. I asked Paul to raise the candle higher, a job to which he gladly obliged. When it was raised up, however, it lost the effect and the wax, hardened before it dropped to my face.

Writhing with pain, I let them finish the job. Boy, did I catch hell when I got home, it took me two days to get the wax off my face!

WHAT DO MOST PEOPLE DO ON A DATE?

On the first date, they just tell each other lies and that usually gets them interested enough to go for a second date.
—Martin, age 10

Before you criticize someone, you should walk a mile in their shoes. That way, when you criticize them, you are a mile away and you have their shoes.—unknown

CHAPTER 7B.

Tank & Timmy Arlet

Tank & Timmy were Smithton Street Gang "recruits" and were younger, but they were my weekend buddies. Mr. & Mrs. Keenan's grandchildren, we usually got together on weekends during school season. But in the spring & summer months, (count them, six of them) they were with me. We did all kinds of things together, play cars, sweeper disc, (see Chapter 12) went to the ducky, but mostly wiffle ball (see Chapter 12 A). I remember, I couldn't wait to be able to drive, so I could take them everywhere I never went.

The two of them were comical when they argued with each other. When it turned into fisticuffs, Tim would stick one hand in his mouth and go at Tank. He would stop him short by holding Tim's head back with one hand and letting him swing away. Tim, by being smaller, would not be able to get a punch in. Tim didn't care, he just kept swinging away with one hand hoping to connect. He never did, however, he would swing at Tank until he was tired, then the argument was over

WHAT WOULD YOU DO ON A FIRST DATE THAT WAS TURNING SOUR?

I'd run home and play dead. The next day I would call all the newspapers and make sure they wrote about me in all the dead columns.—Craig, age 9

If at first you don't succeed, skydiving is not for you.—unknown

CHAPTER 7C.

Tony "Nino" Tusa

Nino (Booza) was different, not a bad different, a good different. He was a mediator. Any time any of us fought, Nino would try to settle the matters himself. He had this crazy habit of making a closed fist motion, wringing his wrist all the time. It caught on to all the girls at Dominick high school.

I remember one basketball game, Dominick scored a basket, all the girls in the entire gym displayed Ninos hand fist motion He was always picked on or teased about it. What I do remember is calling on him to come out and play, only to have his mother tell us of all the chores he had to do first. We gave up on him, went in for the evening, only to find out he came out later when "his chores were done"

He writes:
"I was born on Smithton St. on Sept. 11th, 1949. The house I was born in and house at 3219 Central Ave. where my parents moved when I was a year old are both torn down. My father died when I was eleven years old. My mother became very depressed and did not care where I went and what I did. I quickly gravitated back to Smithton St. although in one sense I never left.

My earliest recollection of friendship was with Rusty since we were first cousins and found ourselves together at family gatherings as early as age two. Jimmy, Paul, Porjy, Mace, Tank, and Timmy came into my life a little further down the road. Although my relationships with these guys are still on solid ground today let me take some time to talk about the relationships with the adults that I also still revere to this day. First and foremost my aunt and uncle, Mr. and Mrs. William Waxler Sr. Rusty's parents, are at the head of the list.

As I said earlier when my father died in 1961, and my mother sort of gave up on things, my aunt and uncle were there to offer guidance and direction. My aunt Eva was at times a taskmaster, which I needed. But my uncle Boobie was also my little league manager who taught me a lot about the game of baseball. Other prominent adults include Mrs. 'E', Jimmy's mom, Mr.and Mrs. Trunick. aunt Maisie, Porjy's mom, and even Mr. and Mrs. Tripoli come to mind. Getting together at Jimmy's to play cards, have a few beers, and chew the fat about old times has been one of the most rewarding experiences for me as of late

I don't see Porjy much, but when I do, I really enjoy him picking on me. Don't tell him I like it! But when it's all said and done, I think we cemented our relationships with one another when we played softball and football together. I could go on and on about my friends but this is already page four. In closing I would like to say that God has blessed me with really great friends! You know you have great friends when you are all over fifty and you're still getting together. The relationships we established as kids has withstood the test of time! Amen. "

I can recall, when Rusty and I were 18 and 19 respectively, Nino worked at GC Murphy's down town.

They were the only retail—outfit who used to sell six-packs of beer in the city. Nino would buy two six packs, bring them out of the store, give one six pack to me, the other one to Rusty, and Rusty and I would drive up to the cemetery, get blasted out of our ever loving minds, and walk around the headstones trying to figure out which one was the oldest.

WHEN IS IT OKAY TO KISS SOMEONE?

When they're rich and famous.—Pam, age 7

CHAPTER 7D.

Rich" Mace" Macik

Mace was one of the invisible gang members, you didn't see him, but he was there occasionally. He was mostly Tank and Timmy's age, so he hung out with them. I remember that he did play all of our outdoor games with us, and then some. Prime example was wiffleball, we had him play the outfield most of the time (out on the street) because he had this line drive throw, and was able to throw out runners quicker than Tank or Timmy.

When he played Boston baked beans (a.k.a. Hide the Belt) we were afraid of getting too rough with him, so whoever had the belt, had to be extra careful when swinging at him, or Paula (his mom) would be knocking at our door. I believe it was him, Georgie Richter, one of the Pivarotti girls, and two other kids, who were the audience for our famous monster show.

He later writes:
"I remember playing wiffle ball in Jimmy's yard when I was about 9 or 10 yrs old. I was a little younger than everybody else. I had to play the outfield which was across the street over the curb and sometimes behind the trees over the hill when the sluggers were up. Your throw to the infield was an uphill throw.

41

We also played football in the street. Mr Leuwickie or the TOKEO YO-YO were always hollering about hitting the telephone lines or the cars. I don't blame them now.

We also played tin can alley and hide the belt. that hurt, I could just imagine the sissy's today getting hit with the belt by the likes of Paul Trunick. There would be a number of lawsuits going on. I always had a good hiding place that nobody ever found me, but I would have to run to home base and hope that Paul would not be the one with the belt.

Another place we played hide the belt was in the cemetery which was a little scarier, it was darker and therefore more dangerous. I remember running and not touching the ground for a while and when I did it was about five foot across the road, I tore my watermelon colored bellbottoms across the knees. I remember drinking in the cemetery on the old dump road when Porjy was AWOL.

He had Leo's old 59 Chevy convertible. Jimmy, Rusty and Paul used to put on horror shows in Jimmy's front room downstairs It was always kind of scary even though we knew who it was. I was scared of the big old butcher knife that they always seemed to have. Jimmy used to hold séances's with the oweji board, the wallpaper used to peel off the ceiling and walls. scary-real scary.

We used to play hide and seek all over Jimmy's mom's house, which I didn't know very well upstairs. I made it to a clothes cupboard up stairs at the top of the stairs some place. There it contained Jimmy's mother's wedding dress, I figured nobody would bother with it, so that became my hiding place,— behind the dress. I always thought that was pretty cool.

I remember playing whiffel ball in the yard, I was playing infield then. Jimmy's sister Linda called down the steps asking someone to zip the back of her dress, I offered. Boy did my hands tremble. She was going out on a date with Art. I think he was president of the Pagan's then.

We used to pull fire drills in Riverview park with Jimmy's 65 Olds con, and JR's 57 t-bird, man was that fun. A

The guy's used to have contest on who could take apart and put back together a 7 millimeter rifle, I think the fastest time was 17 seconds.

We started a Smithton street foot ball team, we hardly had any equipment, I member playing without a helmet. When we kicked the ball off Tank said I got downfield first was because I was always offside but I never got busted for it. The North Side Saints would not play us because our front line was all over 200 lbs. There was one game I always remembered, it was played out North Park. I got drunk the night before. When we got to the park Animal broke out a bottle of Ouzo and I started all over again. What a game. I scored my only TD as a defensive player. We whooped Ass Again."

WHEN IS IT OK TO KISS SOMEONE?

When you're sure they wiped all the germs away
—Philip, age 8

CHAPTER 7E.

Vicki Tripoli

Oh, what a little love triangle we had here, Vicki was the one and only female on Smithton St. that was our age. I liked Vicki, the feelings were not mutual. Vicki liked Rusty, the feelings were mutual. Vicki tried to match me up with her cousin Aggie, there was nothing happening there. Rusty did hook up with her finally, and went out with her two or three times, that's when they tried to hook me up with Aggie. She would not hear of it, she liked the older boys.

I thought I had Vicki hooked one day when I took my guitar to her house and knocked on the door. She answered and told me to wait outside until she was done with her chores. Wild Bill (our nickname for her father), was very strict with her, and would not hear of any shenanigans going on behind his back.

I had to wait outside for about half an hour until she was done. She finally came out, and we both sat on her wall, I serenaded her with my version of (I remember it as if it was yesterday) "Ferry Cross The Mercy" by Gerry And the Pacemakers... Needless to say, she was very impressed," that was beautiful Jim, what was the name of it?" The songs title is mentioned at least four times. I lose.

WHEN IS IT OK TO KISS SOMEONE?

The law says you have to be 21, so I wouldn't want to mess with that.—Curt, age 7

CHAPTER 8.

Break Your Neck Hill

Break Your Neck Hill, was a steep hill leading to Riverview Park with nothing but broken glass from the older kids drinking beer, and breaking the bottles on the rocks. It was called Break Your Neck because they used to use it as a horse path until a horse fell and broke its neck on it. I recall vividly, Rusty, Paul, and I, climbing the hill to go swimming at Riverview pool one day. Deciding halfway up, to getting undressed, and hiding our clothes, shoes and all, just wearing our bathing suits, to avoid the long lines waiting to have their clothes registered. We passed the broken glass, covered our clothes with leaves, and climbed the hill in our bare feet to the pool.

The asphalt road leading to the pool, was very hot indeed, but it was worth it, because the line to get in, was backed up all the way out the door, up the steps, and halfway down the road. We went right in.

We swam all day long, and when it was time to go home, we walked that long road tuckered out. We started down Break Your Neck Hill and smelled a faint odor of burning rubber. We got to where our clothes were covered and couldn't find them,

All we found was a smoldering pile of burnt clothing and tennis shoes!
We were furious and heartbroken all at the same time. A long trip turned longer still, especially trying to walk over broken glass. By the time we got home, our feet were bloody messes. I got hell from my mother for losing my clothes, and I'm sure the other two guys got their fair share too.

WHEN IS IT OK TO KISS SOMEONE?

The rule goes like this: If you kiss someone, then you should marry them and have kids with them. It's the right thing to do.— Howard, age 8

CHAPTER 9.

Paul Trunick's Temper

As I said before, Paul Trunick had a hairpin trigger temper, (that's the best way I can describe it) and he hated being called Juice. (When he was little, he would go to Glassbrenner's pharmacy, and tell Mr. Glassbrenner he wanted juice. Glassbrenner knew what he wanted, but used to think it was cute, he would laugh at young Paul, and Paul hated him for it.

One evening, the three of us, Paul, Rusty and I, were standing in front of my House talking. Ronnie Smith came riding by us on his bicycle, with a smirk on his face. We all knew what he was up to, we just wondered when he would do it. He got to the bottom of Smithton, far enough away (he thought so anyway) if I would gauge the distance, I would say the width of about 10 houses, Ronnie let out a big "JUICE."

Paul wasted no time, he jumped down all seven of my steps with one leap, Rusty and I looked at each other and both thought the same thing, "he'll never catch him." Boy, were we ever wrong, Paul had him before he could reach the width of another house. He threw Ronnie off the bike, took the bike to the nearest telephone pole, and wrapped it around the pole. I can still see, in my mind's eye, Ronnie trying to ride his hobbled bike home, it had a mind of its own I never again doubted the speed nor the strength of Paul Trunick, and the word juice, escaped my vocabulary.

IS IT BETTER TO BE SINGLE OR MARRIED?

I don't know which is better, but I'll tell you one thing. I'm never going to have sex with my wife. I don't want to be all grossed out.—Theodore, age 8

CHAPTER 10.

Porjy" Nut" Retterback

Porjy Retterback, (known as the Nut all around Northside), had a reputation, because he would find a way to get himself into fixes anywhere, anytime. He wasn't afraid of getting into fights with the neighborhood hoodlums, He was really a pussycat with his friends. He hated thieves, I recall one time, he found out one of the neighborhood kids stole something from his room.

He hunted him down (I was with him), smacked him around a couple times (just to teach him a lesson), a bigger fellow, Pork Chop was his name, said to Porjy, "why don't you pick on somebody your own size, like me for instance?" Porjy ran from him at first, but then something inside him made him quit running, Porjy turned around, and beat the shit out of him. Porjy used to say," there's only one man that I was ever afraid of, and that was Gramps."

I was 15, and one evening Porjy came to my house in his 58' Chevy "stick" 3 speed on the floor, Porjy had a crush on Sparkle, and thinking he would get somewhere with her, threw me the keys to his car and told me to "take it for a ride" so I gladly obliged. I got in, started it up, and it sounded like a fire truck. Porjy failed to tell me, that the exhaust system had a leak in it. I didn't give a damn, I was in seventh heaven, I put it in first gear and took off.

In those days, it was rare for a boy my age to know how to drive a "stick". I went down Smithton, back up again to the other end, down Grand Avenue, down Central Ave. to the Dairy Queen lot. I turned around in the lot and headed back home again, up Central, up Grand, back to Smithton. I was in my glory! I parked it and went back into the house to find Porjy and Linda sitting in the kitchen, having home made deep-fried potato chips and pink lemonade. I walked out with Porjy and asked him what he did while I was away. And he said," I listened to you." He told me the exact route I took (the car was that loud). It seems, he was getting nowhere with Sparkle, so he listened to his car.

One of my fondest recollections of Porjy entails me getting a play car dashboard for Christmas one year. Complete with steering wheel, turn signals, ignition turning on and off a little motor, and a gearshift.

I sat in one end of my red wagon, with the dashboard at the other end. Porjy let me "drive" while he pulled me all around the neighborhood.

IS IT BETTER TO BE SINGLE OR MARRIED?

It's better for girls to be single but not for boys. Boys need someone to clean up after them.—Anita, age 9 (bless you child)

CHAPTER 11.

Don "Shultz" Retterback

Don Retterback, known as "Schultz" among the guys because he was younger and used to follow the members of the Cross Gang around, asking for "shorts" of their cigarettes. Hence the name "Shultz" Followed in the shadow of Porjy, where Porjy was a lion, Don was a lamb, soft spoken, quiet. When Porjy got in trouble, Don would usually find a way to get him out of it. I recall one time Porjy was accused of stealing pop from Mikale's five and dime (he didn't of course) but Don smoothed it out with Mr. Mikale.

I also recall, (and he will too, naturally), at the Dairy Queen lot, we were having an argument, I decided that the only way to win, was to fight him.
He was smaller than me, so I figured I had the advantage. Not. We were walking home, I dove for him, he moved out of the way just in time. I missed him, and hit the asphalt and the gravel at the same time. I came up with my face and mouth full of gravel, and a couple of bumps on my noggin. I learned my lesson the hard way, never mess with someone quicker than you.

I had a pocket watch I received from my cousin Barbara Hopper that I cherished. Somehow, Don ended up with it and busted it, I was heartbroken. Don took it to Gramps to see if he could do anything with it.

He did! That Gramps was amazing, he fixed it almost as good as new. It's like Willy and Don used to tell me, "our Gramps can do anything."

HOW WOULD YOU MAKE A MARRIAGE WORK?

Tell your wife that she's beautiful, even if she looks like a truck.—Donald age 7

CHAPTER 11B.

Gramps

Now there's a name that creeps up from the past. Gramps was Czechoslovakian. Although he didn't speak it fluently, he had a slight accent, I don't know if it is the Slovakian nature, but he was very loud and demanding with his voice. Just like my father, If he told you to jump, don't bother asking how far, or how high, just JUMP.

He stood about six-foot two, thin snow white hair, and I don't recall ever seeing him without his bifocals. I'm sure he was a pussycat deep down inside. He lived by himself downstairs in a basement two room apartment of his daughter, Maisie (Porjy and Don's mom) I can recall him being very stocky. All I know is, all the guys on Smithton Street feared him.

He was as strong as an ox, something we found out later. Although he never hit any of us, so we were not able to tell. He was a cook at the local Italian club, and used to arm wrestle people just for the fun of it. We also found out, he never lost. In fact, he used to arm wrestle two or three men at any given time, any given day.

There are two theories to winning an argument with a woman—neither one works

CHAPTER 11C.

Jackie "Smoke" Hunt

What can I say about my childhood friend & cousin except for Music, Music, Music. We went through grade school together inseparable. We sang together in all the school plays, gave the teachers hell, and broke out in fisticuffs every now and then. My earliest, fondest memory of him entailed him and I and Mrs. Sherman (our musical director & third-grade teacher) practicing singing the song "Long Long Ago" over and over again for a school play coming up.

I was to do the lower harmony part, he was to sing the lead. We had it down pact in rehearsal. Come show time, with all those proud parents looking on, I panicked and started singing the lead with him, nobody noticed but Jackie and I and Mrs. Sherman, who just rolled her eyes as if to say," all that rehearsing"

Jackie had a set of Western dolls, probably still does for that matter, that his mother bought him. I would have given my right arm for. They were of: The Lone Ranger, Tonto, Roy Rogers, Dale Evans, Wild Bill Hickock, (I think) complete with horses! I always wanted to play with them, and he said, "no, I want to save them" boy, was he ever smart at his young age, they are probably worth a fortune now.

When the Beatles first came out, we were awestruck. We vowed up and down to be like them. My dad bought me a guitar, Jackie's mom got him his first set of drums, they were beautiful, if my memory serves me right, they were red pearl.
Jackie used to practice religiously, me, on the other hand, I would practice the day of my guitar lessons. He became a spectacular drummer. I became so so on guitar.

After learning some songs, we hooked up with guitar players Al Lipp & Ricky Norris at a party thrown by my then girlfriend Joanie Seifert, in Westview, PA. We formed a little four piece band. I made up the name Cordell's, after seeing Jim Irwin's business card with Cord Printing Company.

Our one & only job was playing a dance at the Bellevue, PA. YMCA. Uncle Harry Kraemer was the coordinator. We only had six songs in our repertoire, we played them over and over. Jackie and I had our differences with music preferences, although, he wanted to play dances, I wanted to play weddings.

I switched from rhythm, to bass guitar, and took over Pepper's job from Pepper & The Red-hots as the lead singing bass player, the Cordells added Pinkie (Don Martin, a bass player) and a couple of horn players, and changed their name to Herman's Marching Band. We went different ways music wise.

Jackie did not grow up on Smithton Street, he moved to Mitchell St. & then to Grand Avenue, although, he did come around every now and then to play with us. He spearheaded a Smithton Street gang softball & football team. The softball team used to play beer games, and never lost. The football team was a wild story, at 245 pounds, I was the smallest guy on the defensive line. I remember buying all the equipment that I needed, and so did the other guys. We only got two teams to play us tackle football. Needless to say, we never lost that neither.

Jackie was a hell of a catcher in little league. He inherited the nickname "Smoke" After Smokey Burgess, the Pittsburgh Pirate catcher at that time. In little league, it was considered quite a feat to throw out a runner going to second base, without bouncing the ball on one bounce.

Smoke was able to throw out the opposing runners without that bounce! Nearly every time, a runner tried to steal base, Smoke would peg him out. He & Nebo (Don Neboresni) were the best two hitters on our Giants team. Any time you needed that base hit, Smoke or Don would pull through. I was proud to be his cousin.

"I just bought a Yorkie. It's the perfect dog for lazy people. You don't have to walk it. Just open the window, hold it out, and squeeze."—Tony Clark

CHAPTER 12.

Rusty "Tic" Waxler

Rusty Waxler, I can't say anything bad about him, because it will blow my cover, he was my best friend at the time. (When he joined the service, Paul and I became close again) He received his nickname from Roy Seers, a black boy who went to school with us and couldn't pronounce his last name. The very first thing that sticks in my mind, when we were kids, Rusty was THE baseball player, he ate, slept, & showered, thinking about baseball. The only problem was, all the playing he did, he had never hit a home run over the fence. He hit inside the park homeruns, however, and plenty over the fence with 1 bounce doubles, but never a homer over the fence.

I'll never forget, I had a dream, I was watching him play in an All-Star game. He hit a high fly to right-center field, he had the wind at his back (I knew that because of the way the flag was flying) in my dream the ball was high enough and far enough to carry it over the fence.

He had hit a home run. Only problem is, as he was rounding first, going to second, he tripped and fell over second base. Even for a dream, it was an embarrassing event. I told him about the dream and he said, "I was just picked to play in the All-Star game Saturday!!!"

Game day came, Rusty was cool as a cucumber, he couldn't let my silly dream interfere with his ball playing ability. His mom took us to the ball field, (she used to love to watch him play) we always got there early, so he could get his warm-ups in. I reminded him about my dream premonition, and he said that if he got a homerun, he would be sure not to trip over second base.

I don't remember much of the game, but I do remember (and I will never forget) him batting in the fourth inning of a six inning game, and hitting a long fly ball to right-center field. It was high enough, and deep enough, to go over the fence. It was his first homerun ever over the fence! Rusty, the team, his mother, and I were ecstatic, I watched him carefully round first base, he slowed down, however, at second base, so as not to "trip". I was relieved, and went out to congratulate him.

The guys will remember playing "sweeper disc baseball" Rusty was out at the dump (our favorite rooting ground) found some cloth "discs" and brought them home. We made up a baseball game using them. The rules were as follows: You start out with a pitcher and a batter, that's all, if you could hit the disc four feet without the pitcher touching it, (it was next to impossible to hit more than four feet) it was a single,

If you hit it eight feet, it was a double, ten feet, a triple. A whopping twenty feet, would be a homerun. If the pitcher caught it in the air, it was all three outs. If he touched any part of it, while in flight, it was an out. If he touched any part of it while rolling, it was an out.

The batter never leaves the batter's box. You kept tabs of the runners in your heads (both pitcher, and batter). You played nine inning games, and kept score in your heads also

Another wild time is riding in his 57' Thunderbird (classic car) two seater, late at night through Riverview Park, we were both shit faced drunk. We were cruising about 30 mph, 15 over the speed limit, it was a foggy night, you couldn't see your hand in front of your face, the road was winding, it was a one way road, and we were headed THE OPPOSITE WAY! I don't know whose idea it was, or why we did it, all I know is, it was just crazy! We could have been killed if another car was coming the other way. There was just room for one car on that road.

He used to ride around town, stopping at green lights, waiting till they turned red, then driving right through them. He would complain about his brother doing the same thing. I asked him why then did he do it? And his answer was, "in case my brother is coming the other way!"

He writes:

"Nut, Tic, Ehr, Smoke, Shultz, Juice, Bozo, Wall Balls, Tokyo YoYo, Lump, Big Yode, Little Yode, Eagle Beak, The Eyes and Ears of the World, Sausage, Nino, Tutsi, Mace, Booza, and Lead Head. That's just a few of the nicknames we all knew in our childhood growing up on Smithton Street. I know that just about everyone thinks they had some real characters growing up, I am sure of it!

What was it like growing up on Smithton Street? I am glad you asked. Well, as any group of kids did, we lived for summer vacation. The typical day would start with everyone meeting on the street at about 8 o'clock. That's me, Rusty, Porjy, Jimmy Ehrhardt, Jimmy Long, Paul, and any one else we could muster. We would take our bikes, and put our gloves on the handlebar. We usually had one or two baseballs and a couple of bats that were usually broke once and had a nail and some electrical tape holding them together. Then our trek would start to the Ducky (see Chapter 20), which was our ball field about a half mile way, in Riverview Park.

The trip started, and we could not wait to find out the answer to the big Question. Was the field open? You see, sometimes the enemy, which was the kids from Perrysville Ave. would get there before us.

This was the problem. We would then ask if they would play against us in a game. If they refused, we would ask to play with them. If they refused, we would unload a bunch of insults, obscenities, and usually some good ribbing usually led by Paul, as he was the biggest.

There was an area just below the Ducky, and just below the swings, where we could improvise and play a game, but on a smaller scale, and with special rules to cover trees and obstacles. Nonetheless we played. One good thing, was that we were by the water fountain. This meant that the boys from Perry would have to walk past to get a drink, at which time, we abused them. When the game was over, we would jump on our bikes for a great ride home. You see, the trip home was all downhill, and we could make it almost home without pedaling.

We would all go home and eat lunch, change, and get ready for the next part of our day.

That was about a 1 mile walk up Break Your Neck through Riverview Park to the pool which opened at one.

We went to the pool just about every day. The exception was on days of Little League games, as the coaches frowned upon it, you will be tired.

They would even check your eyes to see if you went. There was no Murine in those days, and chlorine eyes were unmistakable. The games we played at the pool were as much fun as getting a glimpse of the girl getting undressed through the usually open windows. Speaking of girls, the pool was responsible for some of us getting our first real girlfriends.

Time to go home for supper. The walk was always longer on the way home, I guess the coaches were right, cause I was tired! After supper the options were many. We would play a big game of wiffleball.

Sometimes we would play a release or Tin Can Alley. Let's not forget Hide and Seek, Rundown, or Red Rover. Maybe it was a night to chase Paul in the cemetery in a good old game of monsters. In either case, it was a blast, and we went full tilt until it was time to go home. The memories of these days will live in my heart and mind forever. The friendships created are lifelong, and I feel like something that makes we were all meant to be together.

People came and went, but the true group of Smithton Street, will never be forgotten. Thanks for the memories, I guess Brian Adams summed it up the best in his song, "Summer of 69." Those summers seemed to last forever
Those Were The Best Days Of My Life!!!!!!!

Another crazy thing we did, was sled ride on the icy roads. We just couldn't do normal sled riding, no, we had to Corvair ride! And that is where we drive Rusty's 65 Corvair through the snowy & icy streets while two of us held on to the back bumper of the car!

His brother, Butch lived in Point Breeze with his wife Bert (short for Roberta) and kids, Stevie and Susie. Rusty and I used to baby-sit them, I was in heaven because the house was so huge. It had about eight rooms and "I had never been in a house that big before. It had an intercom system in it that we used to play with. And a big basement. You could probably fit a Mack truck down there (18 wheeler no less)

I was a snoop in my younger days. One night, I was going through the drawers of Butch's night stand and found a gun,, I closed the drawer instantly and told Rusty. He asked me to show it to him and told me I should stay the f—k out of Butch's things. Needless to say, that was the end of my snooping days

"A Russian psychologist is selling a video that teaches you how to test your dog's IQ. Here's how it works: if you spend $12.99 for the video, your dog is smarter than you." —Jay Leonard

CHAPTER 12B.

Wiffleball

Wiffleball was a strong favorite in the neighborhood, almost every night after dinner, most of the neighborhood would gather to play. Me, Tank, Timmy, Rusty, Porjy, Don, Tony Tusa, & Pepper.

We would usually have three or four to a team, depending on who showed up, play in the little lot beside my house, and I mean little. We would use the apple tree as first base, a rock as second base, a porch column as third base, and another rock as home. I ride past that yard frequently, and wonder how the hell we all fit a baseball field in there.

One game I remember well, Tony was rounding second after a double he hit and tried stretching it to a triple. He came to third at a full steam and grabbed hold of the porch column but forgot to let go. It dismantled in his hand and that portion of the roof came sagging down. We quickly put it back together the best we could, but as I recall that part of the roof never did look right again. I was the homerun King, that and a quarter would probably get us a candy bar.

You know you are a dog lover if Your hungry hubby comes home from work, lifts the cover of the pan on the stove and says, "Is this people food or dog food?"

CHAPTER 12C.

Pepper

It seemed like Pepper was with me almost as long as my friends. He was a little black-and-white mongrel that I received during my stay at the hospital at six years old (see Chapter 12 D.) He lived to be 17, which is pretty good for a dog life. He followed me everywhere, and did everything with me.

He ran the bases with me during our wiffleball games, and gave me away when we played hide and seek. He was an excellent companion, he would speak, give you his left or right paw (and he knew the difference) rollover and play dead, and helped you clean off your plate of broccoli. If I could take any day back in the world, it would be the day that I took him his last trip to the Humane Society. I didn't know that you could request to take the ashes with you for a decent burial.

Never feed the cat anything that doesn't match the rugs—
Author unknown

CHAPTER 12D.

My Accident.

When I was five years old, I was playing in a playground at a picnic my fathers company held. I was playing on one of those manual merry-go-rounds and didn't notice that there was a hole in the center board of the ride. My foot went into the hole and I started screaming. Taking it as a fun scream, the kids pushed it faster, and I screamed even louder. When they finally slowed down, and I continued screaming, they knew something was wrong.

My father, and his friends, came running over to see what was the matter. When they caught the problem, they lifted me out and saw that my foot was hanging by a mere piece of skin (yech!) I remember them loading me into one of the gentleman's station wagon, rushing me to Ohio Valley General hospital and that's all I remembered until I woke up in a hospital room. There was a cast on my foot covering the leg halfway up.

The doctor told my mother, that he tried a new medical procedure, it was called skin grafting. It is the process of taking skin from different parts of the body and applying or grafting it to the affected part of the body.

My mother later told me that the doctor told her that I was "one of the first skin grafting patients in Pennsylvania!" To this day, that foot has always been stronger than my original, dominant left foot.

After the cast came off, I remember motoring room to room on my wheelchair meeting patients left and right, while at the same time terrorizing nurses and doctors, and anyone else who got in my path. I got to be known as "that little demon in the wheelchair." That year, I spent my sixth birthday in the hospital, and received Pepper (see 12 C.) as a birthday gift. To my recollection, one of the best damn birthday gifts I ever received.

"My mom and dad didn't want to move to Florida, but they turned sixty and that's the law."

CHAPTER 13.

Boston Baked Beans

Boston baked beans (a.k.a. Hide the belt) usually played at night.

You pick a player to be it, (known as the hider) to hide the belt. He hidesit, (he wraps it the around the bumper of a car) while everybody closes their eye's.

When he finishes hiding it, he yells out, "Boston Baked Beans" we all open our eyes and try to find the belt. The player that is it, tells the closest player to the belt, whether he is warm or cold. I.e. Jimmy is warm (he is by the car) so everybody goes to the car to search for the belt. Now the hider yells out, "Porjy is hot!"

Porjy spies the belt, but waits until everybody is close enough to him (he wants to beat as many kids senseless as possible with the belt.) When he feels the time is right, he grabs the belt, starts swinging it and hits as many kids as possible at one time.

He takes advantage of the slowest runner, and starts swatting. There is a penalty, however, for hitting someone with the buckle end of the belt.

Such was the case, of the day that we were playing in the "Cemey" (Cemetery), and I found the belt and Don Retterback at the same time.

In my haste to start swatting, I grabbed the wrong end of the belt, and started swinging at Don, he fell over a tombstone, I showed no mercy. I just kept swatting. He held his hand up in self defense, and got his finger broke.

Rules are, the person who is hit, gets to swat the hitter (if you will) on the bottom, five times with the buckle side of the belt. Don showed no mercy either, he swung as hard as he could, broken finger and all. So good old Don, got his revenge. He still has a broken finger, and I still have marks on my ass. Pretty barbaric isn't it?

My tire was bumping
I thought it was flat
When I looked at the tire
I noticed your cat...Sorry.

CHAPTER 13B.

To the Dump

As mentioned before, one of our favorite hangouts was the dump. We would find all kinds of (treasures) junk there, old bottles, broken toys, bent Hula Hoops and slinkys...we would find, What? What's that you say? You don't know what a slinky is? It is as a tight wound spring that made some hapless guy a millionaire selling it to mindless brain dead kids, (Yours truly included) to keep them amused for hours trying effortlessly to make it walk down steps.

Back to the dump, one day while rummaging through the (treasures) junk, Rusty and I found a bunch of 16 mm films. Half of them marked "Travel," while the other half were unmarked. We took them home with us knowing full well, that we did not have a projector to show them.
Rusty took his chances, by calling his brother, who also collected (treasures) junk to ask him if by chance, he had a 16 mm projector.

He said he did, and was just about to throw it out when we called. We said we wanted it, and would he be so kind as to bring it the next time he visited his mother. He said he would, and it happened.

His brother brought a bunch of his old movies, Our Gang, Hop along Cassidy, Tom Mix. We took the projector to Rusty's room for a Premier screening, Little did we know what those films had in store for us.

We watched all of his brother's movies, and put the "Travel" ones in, only to find a bunch of boring documentaries, soundless documentaries at that. When we put the unmarked ones in, much to our surprise, NUDIES!!! Yes dear people, films of nude girls. Full frontal nudity at that, Will wonders ever cease? Here we are, just barely in our teen's, never seeing full frontal nudity before, drooling at women from the early 1900s, frolicking around in their birthday suits, teasing the men with the handlebar mustaches.

The light from the projector was not strong enough to cast a clear image onto the screen, so we decided to switch the 75 W bulb to a 150 W bulb. Needless to say, the heat from the bulb started to melt the cellophane film. We couldn't have that, so we decided to switch bulbs again and one of us had the brainy idea of looking straight into the lens to get a close up view, DUH! Picture this: staring into a magnifying glass, with 75 W of light behind the lens, it's a wonder we didn't go blind!

The next thing to break down, was the cable that turns the take-up reel. Both excited and nervous as could be, we started running around the house searching for something to suffice.
Rusty's mother said to him, "what are you two up to?" We both answered in stereo, "NOTHING." And kept searching. Rusty came upon some gum bands, for all you non-Pittsburghers out there that's Pittsburgheese for rubber bands.

We stuck the rubber bands if you will, on the projector, and we were ready to roll.

Rusty found half a bag of potato chips, and we grabbed two pops from the fridge, with the full box of rubber bands, we spent the afternoon taking turns staring into the lens, burning our retinas, and watching our first batch of nudie movies.

You had your bladder removed
And you're on the mends
I bought you some flowers
And a box of Depends.

CHAPTER 14.

To Work With Dad

My father, to make up for quality time he was missing with me, almost always took me to work with him on Saturdays. He was the main foreman in a carpet and linoleum distributing warehouse. He let me drive the forklift around the warehouse! it was the highlight of my life at age 9. Rusty and I went to work with him one day. We ran around the warehouse playing hide and seek. I remember Rusty hiding in between a stack of vertical carpeting.

He bumped one, which in turn created a domino effect of carpeting, we had carpets everywhere, all over the floor. Needless to say, that was the last time my dad took me to work with him for a while.

Deja Moo: The feeling that you've heard this bullshit before.

CHAPTER 15.

Ouija Boards & Wally Arrives

My house was haunted, there was no doubt about that. Everybody witnessed strange goings on. We had Ouija Boards that actually moved on their own, doors that opened and closed on their own, lights that went on and off on their own. The Ouija board even gave us a name for the ghost, it was Wally! Wally made himself present at the most inopportune times, mostly at night, when you wanted to sleep. Lights would come on, and then go off. The stereo would come on, and then off again.

I remember like clockwork, every Saturday night, while Paul and I watched Chiller Theater, Sparkle and Sissy Retterback, (Porjy & Don's sister, see Chapter 10 & 11), would break out the Ouija board, and start asking questions. Wally had an infatuation with the time of 9:40 p.m. Every evening, the clock would stop at that time, until we had to physically unplug it, and plug it back again.

One evening, while playing with the Ouija board, it foretold us many things that came true. It told us that my father's car would be involved in a terrible accident with fatalities. We were horrified, we didn't know whether to believe it or not, or whether my father would believe it or not, we called him anyway and told him about the Ouija board. He shrugged it off, and told us to "stop playing with the god damn thing."

We found out the next day, however, he lent his car out to Jim, a fellow coworker, There was a terrible accident, a car pulled out on Jim, and crossed two lanes, while he was going 60 miles an hour. It totaled my father's car, and there were fatalities on the other driver's side.

My father instantly became a firm believer in Wally. Wally also foretold us about my father's plan to become engaged to his second wife, we never told him that one though

Your daughter's a hooker
So it spoiled your day
Look at the bright side
She's a very good lay.

CHAPTER 16.

Wally's Shenanigans

Another evening, while the gang was over playing a game of poker, we heard a loud THUMP, THUMP, THUMP coming from outside the kitchen door. We opened the door in time to see a large pop bottle making its way up the stairs towards us! We quickly closed the door, and the noise stopped.

At the same time, we heard in the hallway, adjacent to the kitchen, another noise, we gathered up enough courage to open the door in time to see a bag of my Mother's potatoes fly across the hall, and down the steps to the first-floor apartment. Losing potatoes along the way. That was enough for my company to see, they hi-tailed it home, leaving Sparkle and I to deal with Wally on our own.

My Mother had a bedroom adjacent to that same hallway that she never used. She said she preferred sleeping on the couch, it was more comfortable, but we think that Wally inhabited it and scared her out of it. The lighting was poor in that hallway when it was on, so we were extremely cautious when going to the bathroom through that same hallway, so as not to disturb Wally, or he would create havoc.

When the light was off, and it usually was, the switch was behind a huge coat rack, and we didn't want to spend any time looking for it, we would fly through that scary dark hallway to the bathroom.

One evening, when Chiller Theater was over, (I actually made it through the second movie without falling sleep) Paul and I heard a huge crash, coming from somewhere downstairs.

We looked at each other in shear terror, after being motionless for several seconds, Paul finally said to me, "what the hell was that?" I said I didn't know, part of me relieved that he actually heard it too, and the other part of me too terrified to move. We're talking some serious bullshit here. We finally gathered up enough courage to go downstairs (we were watching the show in my bedroom in the attic).

With Paul in the lead, and me, glued to his back, we went straight to the kitchen, everything was in order. We grabbed two butcher knives from the kitchen drawer for protection, and proceeded to check the rest of the house.

We checked the living room, everything was OK. Then we made our way to that dreaded hallway. Paul opened the door to the hallway, with me still glued, he proceeded down the steps to the empty apartment downstairs, with me still glued.

He opened the door to the downstairs apartment, turned to me and said," will you give me some f—king space?" (Paul was always to the point). I kindly obliged. The kitchen in the downstairs apartment, was the first room we entered. It was there that we discovered the culprit.

The previous tenant must have forgotten his silverware in the drawer, for there it was, all over the floor, Wally is probably still laughing to this day!

Heard your wife has left you
How despondent you must be
But don't fret about it
She's moved in here with me

CHAPTER 17.

Wally Strikes In the Afternoon

Wally made his presence known during the day, too. One afternoon, while we were playing whiffle ball outside in the yard, we heard a loud scream coming from inside the house. We all ran up the steps, opened the door, just in time to see my mother's bedroom door, slam shut.

Needless to say, we all ran down the steps at the same time, the gang all ran home leaving me to deal with Wally on my own again. Another afternoon, while I was practicing on my guitar (amplifier and all), the stereo came on louder than my amplifier, for no reason at all. Being used to Wally and all his tricks, I nonchalantly turned the stereo off and proceeded playing my guitar.

Once again, the stereo came on again louder than me. Irritated, I turned the stereo off once again and resumed my Carnegie Hall performance. One more time the stereo came on even louder than before. Not to be outdone, I just turned the volume up on my amplifier to try to drown it out.

*Just then, the phone rang, it was Frank Inskipt from down
the street, "what are you f—king nuts, turn that f—king thing
down, I can't hear myself think."*

*You totaled your car
You can't remember why
Must have been right after you drank
That case of Bud Dry?*

CHAPTER 18.

Linda, Ring Baloney & Pink Lemonade

As I said, my father left home when I was nine, leaving my Mother, Linda, and I, to deal with family matters. My mother did a wonderful job of raising us. Linda (my father called her Sparkle Plenty), did an outstanding job taking care of me and family problems that arose when my mother was not at home. She took care of cooking, and cleaning the house.

She once made us a ring baloney for dinner, (what is a ring baloney, you ask?) It is a long strip of oversize hotdog that usually always splits and turns inside out when you cook it. She would try numerous times to make it without that happening, to no avail. I used to tell people that Linda could do wonders with small meals. She also always made pink lemonade for us, and we always drank it, no matter how sweet or sour it was, and it was always so delicious.

My father was very stern, every kid in the neighborhood, including me, was afraid of him. I recall bringing home a report card with a "D" on it. He was furious, he chased me around the house and up the steps to my room, he chased me around my wraparound banister, screaming at me, I thought he was going to kill me! He never did catch up with me, he did however. threaten to ground me for a month if I ever brought home another "D"

He only took us a few times for a ride through Riverview Park in the evening, Sparkle and him used to count lovebirds, I always looked into the trees, I never did see any lovebirds. My Mother had to beg him to take us to get ice cream at Dairy Queen, he never did oblige.

He had time for his friends though, any time his friends would call, he was gone. My mother used to say, " Angel away, Devil at home." He was very popular with his friends, they used to tell me how good he was. He never proved it at home. All he did, was sit in his favorite chair, read the newspaper, and fall asleep.

"The problem with the designated driver program, it's not a desirable job, but if you ever get sucked into doing it, have fun with it. At the end of the night, drop them off at the wrong house."

CHAPTER 19.

My Mother, Mrs. E.

*"There is a destiny that makes us brothers
None goes his way alone
all we send into the lives of others
Comes back into our own"
Edwyn Markham*

*"God grant me the serenity to accept the things I cannot change,
to change the things I can, and the wisdom to know the difference"
The Serenity Prayer*

Two of my Mother's favorite sayings, one of her boyfriends was a reformed alcoholic. "

Born Ruth Dorothea Natoli 20th of November of '23 her mom died when she was 15, and her Dad went into the Navy, she was forced to live with different aunts and her best friend throughout her teen years. She had to quit school in 12th grade because of lack of clothes. At 17 she went to work full-time at

Steel City Electric (an electrical plant) on an assembly line until she was 21. She met my dad through my Uncle Jack (Jackie Hunt's father), married him & had Linda and I.

When we were very young, she had time for us. She would take us for walks to the Ducky (a little grove in Riverview Park), to play on the swings. As I stated before, my father left home when I was nine & she had to work two jobs to hold the house together.

The guys remember her as "Mrs. E," I think she was one of their favorites, she loved having them around. They were her "family." It was nothing for her to find six or seven bodies sprawled out on the living room floor on any given Saturday or Sunday morning. Watching Deputy Dawg, Mighty Mouse, was it Snaggletooth or Snagglepuss (Exit...Stage Right)? I believe they both said the same thing!.

Someone taught me how to make a hangman's noose, and I thought it was the coolest thing. I made one, and hung it in the downstairs empty apartment. She came home from work and found it hanging there, you would have thought that somebody was occupying it, with the fuss that she made. I was grounded for a week. I didn't even get my hangman's noose back!

She was always 39, till the day she passed, and she always had a little dance she would do when somebody asked Ruthie how old she was. She loved music & musicals especially the King and I. Every time it came on, you would find her glued to the TV. For her birthday one year, we took her to see the play. She was ecstatic, it's all she talked about for weeks.

She had a pair of binoculars she got as a gift one year, and she was in seventh Heaven. She used them exclusively, so we kept getting her gifts of plays and musicals. Nothing pleased her more. When she passed in September of 1990, I inherited the binoculars, and have been using them to this day.

CHAPTER 19B.

Mom's Illness.

One day, while attending Mountain Craft Days in Somerset County with my mother, she began acting strange. Very lethargic, walking very slowly, trying hard to keep up with us. She finally stopped, laid down in the grass, and went to sleep. I was stunned. Not knowing what to do, I left her lay there, and stood with her sleeping in the grass. She napped for about 40 minutes.

When she woke, very gently she said to me "I'm not feeling very good." With that said, she threw up. Not once, but many times. Each time, the one more fierce than the previous one, until she finally said to me, "I think I need to see a doctor" It was then I knew something was terribly wrong, as long as I have been around her, I have never seen her go to a doctor.

She worked at St. John's General Hospital, so she had no problem getting an appointment. Dr. Brenner was his name, and he had a good reputation. All symptoms pointed to gallbladder problems, so they operated on her for that in the fall of 1988.

After the operation, the doctor pulled Linda and I aside, and told us the disturbing news, "while we were removing your *mother's gallbladder, we discovered a mass wrapped around her pancreas, it's very big and inoperable."*

"We could try the Whipple procedure: designed to remove the head, and neck of the pancreas as well as the majority of the duodenum and it is the most commonly performed cancer-directed operation for pancreatic cancer."
"Although it is used in only 9% of patients, your mothers mass would not warrant us to do that, it is wrapped around too many vital organs. It pains me to have to say this, but I can only give her about six months."

Linda and I were shocked to say the least, we never in our wildest dreams thought it to be cancer. She moved in with Linda, and almost immediately started a combination treatment of chemo & radiation to try to kill the cancer cells that were rapidly invading her body. They must have done something right, because six months came and went and mom was still around, although I must say the therapy treatments were taking their toll.

She never did lose any hair, but she did lose weight. Another six months came and went and still she was her jovial self, she seemed to be feeling better, except for the treatments knocking her for a loop, you'd never know she had the big C.
Another five months, and they stopped the radiation because of the beating her body was taking. It was after that, we noticed a major change in her, the weight that she had gained, she was now losing. She was very lethargic again, not wanting to eat. And anything she did eat, all came back up again. Dr. Brenner told us the reason, "your mothers cancer has now spread to her liver, this time, rest assured she only has a month

or two tops. He was right, she passed in September of 1990. 1 1/2 years from the time he diagnosed her.

She made use of having her time by going to Florida with Evis, (a name I had given to Edith as a toddler) her long time friend, and Vince, Edith's husband.

Nothing in the known universe travels quicker than a bad check.

CHAPTER 20.

The Ducky & Little League Baseball

The Ducky was in a part of Riverview Park that had a little playground with a swing set and a ball field. We used to play Little League ball there. We had a small league with four teams; the Braves, Pirates, Giants, and Cards. I started off playing for the Braves, and was traded to the Giants. I wasn't a very good player, I was very clumsy. I played in the outfield, the guys used to chide me, and accuse me of tripping over the homerun chalk line.

I'll never forget, one game our team was down one run, there were two outs in the bottom of the sixth, I was at bat with a man on second. Sparkle was keeping score. The fans (all 12 of them) were silent, I let the first pitch go, it was a strike, there was so much tension in the air, you could have cut it with a knife.

The second pitch was a ball, by a long shot, even I, clumsy Jim, could tell it was a ball (way outside). The third pitch, was also a ball, the crowd was still silent, even the birds stopped chirping. The next pitch, was low and away, too far for me to

hit, but, thinking that I could hit it, I swung anyway. Strike two.
I was behind in the count,

I didn't have much time to study the next pitch, however, it
was a fastball, again low and away. Only this time it was closer
to the plate, I swung with all my might, I connected. It soared
to center field, over the centerfielder's head, and bounced in
front of the homerun chalk line.
I had hit a ground rule double to win the baseball game!
Everybody congratulated me, all the fans, and the coaches on
both sides. It will be an awesome day at the Ehrhardt
household. I couldn't wait to tell my father about the event, I
ran home as fast as I could.

I got home and told my mother about it, and she remarked
how proud of me she was and that my father would be dropping
by. I went outside to play and waited for him to come. He got to
our house just around dinnertime, as soon as he got out of the
car I blindsided him and told him about the double I hit to win
a game.
His remark to me was, "I heard about it, I also heard, that
it wasn't hit very hard".

Seen on the back of a bikers shirt
"If you can read this, the bitch fell off"

CHAPTER 21.

Evil Knievil vonEhrhardt

In a rare instance, when I was 12, my father took me to West View to visit a friend. I went outside to hang out with his 16-year-old son, who had a motorbike. After a while, the boy told me that in West View, you did not have to be 16, nor have a license, to drive a motorbike (boy, was I ever naïve) I didn't know if he was kidding or not, but I took him up on it.

I was thrilled, I got on the bike, started it up, and took to it instantly. I rode all over the place, through the streets, up and down hills. I ran a stop sign, and smack dab into the side of a moving car. I was fine, the bike was fine, but I had knocked the rearview mirror off of the car. The man got out of the car, checked to see if I was all right, and said to me, "how old are you?"
I told him, and he said to me, "didn't you know it is illegal to drive a motor vehicle without a license?" I told him what the boy had told me, and he said to me seriously," where are your parents?" (I was really in trouble now) I rode with him to the house where my father was. He told my father what had happened, and if looks could kill, they would have been holding services for me the next day.

My father offered to pay for anything that needed fixed, and the man said that would be fine. As it turned out, the car was an unmarked police car for West View police, and the man, was an plainclothes police officer who I ended up paying for the mirror myself out of my paper route money

"I want to die in my sleep like my grandfather...
Not screaming and yelling like the passengers in his car..."

CHAPTER 22.

The "F" Word and Our 55 Olds

My mother (God rest her soul) bought us our first car for $40. It was a 1955 Oldsmobile, it made a Sherman Tank look like a toy. It was an awesome piece of machinery, only problem was, not one of us had a license! I remember having to get somebody with a license to drive us in our car anywhere we wanted to go. Any time that happened, I was excited. One time however, I was too excited, Paul, Sparkle, and I were taking a ride to Riverview Park. Paul was going to teach her how to drive (she was 20, I was 15) she also had no permit.

We were headed out Woods Run Avenue, just the three of us, with Paul driving, Sparkle was in the passenger seat, and I was in the backseat. I was in my glory, my best friend, my sister, and I.

Caught up in the moment, forgetting where I was at, and who was in the car, I let the immortal words fly, "man, this f—ker can really kick ass!" (In those days, it was a terrible thing for a boy my age to talk like that in front of a girl) Paul's mouth dropped, Sparkle screamed, "JIMMY!" Boy did I catch hell when I got home.

Wife to husband, "I'd like to go to a place that I've never been before"
Husband to wife, "Try the kitchen."

CHAPTER 22B.

My Honey

When I was 15, a Junior in high school, I saw her. It was love at first sight. (For me anyway) I don't remember what school she transferred from, or where she came from for that matter, but there she was, dark brown hair, bangs (I loved bangs) deep piercing blue eyes, beautiful legs (I was a leg man) and innocent as all get out. I can still see her now, going class to class, oblivious to me.

I found out her name, Maggie, from an acquaintance of both of ours, Judy. Judy attended grade school with her. I also found out, that she grew up on Brighton Road only blocks from my house on Smithton Street (go figure). Her friends were Judy, Mary Lou, Kathy, and Cyc (her sister). With the help of Judy, our group of guys started palling around with their group.

It wasn't long before they were pairing us off, Judy with Nino, Jack with Mary Lou, Rusty with Kathy, and me with Cyc. Leaving no one for Maggie. That didn't last long however, Judy & Tony never hit it off. Rusty and Kathy didn't work, (the feelings were not mutual). Cyc and I didn't last either (Cyc had eyes for somebody else, just when I was starting to like her) Maggie had eyes for Rusty Rusty's feelings at that time were mutual. And so they became a team.

So it was, the only two relationships that were cemented in the whole deal was Jack and Mary Lou & Rusty and Maggie. Until that is, fickle Rusty no longer wanted Maggie, and brushed her off. Time for Harpo to come to the rescue! I took advantage of the whole situation, and lended a sympathetic ear. That did the trick, she was very responsive, and we started going steady in 1968 (September 7, to be exact), when I was 17.

We dated pretty strong at first, six nights a week. And then we cooled off to five nights. And then to four and three nights, which seemed to be working out great for a while. We called for a vacation away from each other for a while when we saw things were getting a little too old. That worked great! We were grateful to start seeing each other again.

What did we do on our dates you ask? Although we were forbidden by her mother, we went to the passion pit (the local drive in) on weekend evenings and actually watched the movies! We did have dilemmas, however, it seems that every time we went to a drive in movie, I would get a flat tire. One night, I got two flat tires! On weekend afternoons, and some early evenings, we went to North Park to feed the ducks!

In the fall of '68, I took her to her Federation dance and we attended my Junior prom. The following year '69, we attended my senior prom & her Junior prom. And then in '70, it was her senior prom. (Lots of Tux's & Gowns) Maggie made her own gowns, and most of her clothes for that matter.

Bumper sticker seen on car
"Your kid may be an honor student but you're still an
IDIOT!"

CHAPTER 23.

Cruisin in my 63' Olds Cutlass

When I was 17, my dad bought me a car for graduation. It was a 63' Oldsmobile Cutlass blue convertible. Man it was sweet, it was only a little six-cylinder four speed on the floor, but it was really quick. Not knowing any better, I used to race everybody, giving it the pounding of a lifetime. I always lost, whether it was me as a driver, or that the car was just not as quick as I thought. But it always withstood the beatings I gave it.

What it didn't withstand one day, was the day that Porjy was driving it, and while trying to "lay rubber," he blew out the rear-end. I found a used one at Raida's junkyard in Millvale for $75 (Porjy picked up the tab) All I remember is, it was freezing bitter cold, with snow on the ground, and it kept snowing. You would lay a bolt or a nut on the ground, and instantly lose it in the snow.

We worked diligently in the snow to try to keep warm by moving, to no avail, our hands and fingers were numb. (It was impossible to work with gloves on). After three hours of sheer agony, we were on the road again. Ready to race and blowout another rear-end

Bumper sticker seen on car "Sometimes I wake up grumpy; Other times I let her sleep"

CHAPTER 24.

Wild Trip in My 66' Opal

I also had a 66' Opal Cadet (a brand now obsolete) that I was quite proud of. It had a five-speed manual transmission that was a thrill to drive. In those days, people held you in awe if you could drive a "stick" I swore, at the time that it could go anywhere and do anything, and Jim Toomey, our trusted eccentric mechanic, confirmed my beliefs by telling me, "that car could probably come down the hill from the Cemetery to Smithton St." Guess what Jim Ehrhardt did?, you got it!

I started on Cemetery Road and cut my wheels left to start down the hill, with Tank and Tim Arlet following on each side of the car. It was a steep hill, untraveled before, and I was scared shitless, but I knew I could do it. The guys would clear any debris from under the car, mainly tree stumps and brush, with their trusty picks, shovels, and axes. Let me tell you, that hill was steep!

I was halfway down, and the car got stuck, the guys went to work (I give them a lot of credit) they dug me out, and I started rolling again. I made it a little bit further and got stuck again, so I shifted to low gear, got myself out, and made it all the way to Smithton St.!

Advice for the day: If you have a lot of tension and you get a headache, do what it says on the aspirin bottle: "Take two aspirin" and "Keep away from children."—Author Unknown

CHAPTER 25.

My "Hat" And My' 66' Caddie

I had a 66' Cadillac Fleetwood I paid $300 for, it was sweet, it had everything imaginable for that time. Power everything, seats, steering, door locks, windows, tilt wheel, automatic dimmer control, the steering wheel used to go in and out. And the stereo, man the stereo was awesome. You were hit with sound from everywhere, there were speakers in the doors, below the dashboard, above the dashboard, and behind the rear bench seat.

I also had a black leather sport hat that I never parted with, I was so proud of that hat, it went with me wherever I went, everything revolved around it. I was even accused of sleeping with it, (which I never did). I had it on one evening and let Rusty drive my Cadillac, I road shotgun with Tony"Nino" Tusa in back.

We were riding through Shadyside and I'll never forget, we decided to give the air-conditioner a break and had the windows down. I was eyeing up some girls, walking down the street, I even stuck my head out the window to get a closer look. It was then Rusty yelled out, "WHAT DO YOU THINK OF MY

HAT?" the girls turned to see who was yelling, and I melted dead in my seat. One of the most embarrassing moments ever.

"I may be fat, but you're really ugly—I can lose weight!"

CHAPTER 26.

Targeted Beetle

I had a 69' Volkswagen convertible that I swear had a target sign painted on its back.

Hitter #1—was a darling elderly couple, I'll say John and Mary (mainly because their real names escape me) John was apologetic to the hilt, he would not stop apologizing until I told him it was okay.

He said the main reason he hit me was that Mary would not stop nagging him, and he could not pay attention to his driving. Mary stayed in the car, while John tried to iron things out.

I had the car towed to my neighbor Hogan's house, who specialized in Volkswagen repair, (thank heaven for small favors) he charged me $200 it was a small repair, plus the cost of the new trunk lid $300, total bill $500, charged to Johns insurance company.

Hitter #2—a teenage boy, I will call him Brian, who just got his license, again he was very apologetic. He said the reason he wasn't paying attention was because he was, " playing with the radio knobs." Back to Hogan, mechanic's charge $300 new *trunk lid $300 total bill $600 charged to kid playing with radio knobs. Insurance company*

Hitter #3—car full of nuns, trying to occupy the same parking place as me at Allegheny Center Mall parking lot, I'll call the driver Sister Mary Delirious, because that's what she was, she was trying to describe for me, with her arms all flinging this way and that, which way she was going to, and which way she was coming from. She said the reason she hit me, the other nuns would not keep quiet long enough for her to concentrate.

Back to Hogan, mechanic's charge $900, new trunk lid $300, total bill $1200, charged to Sister Mary Delirious insurance company. I decided to sell the car after a month, I figured the Almighty one would be the next one in line to hit it, and I wasn't taking any chances on where I'd end up.

Man to woman standing in check out line behind her, "I'll bet your single" woman to man, "you say that because of my small grocery list?" Man to woman, "no, because you're ugly!"

CHAPTER 27.

My Buddy, John" Lump" Orman

John Orman, (a.k.a. Lump, Lump a coal). Now there's a name from the past, Lump, was goofy, he got that way from setting bowling pins one day, someone accidentally threw a ball, a pin jumped up and hit him in the head. He was about 5.4 inches tall, and weighed about 120 pounds soaking wet. He was an older man who used to walk his dog up and down the street yelling, "258, you figure it out" or" Wall ball's" (his name for Jim Toomey, as mentioned in the introduction)

He had a problem one day, his kitchen light bulb burnt out, and he came up the street to tell me about it, but all he could muster was," Yo Jim, lights out." I knew exactly what he wanted. I went down to his house to replace his light bulb, I had done it numerous times before. Only this time was different.

I opened a counter drawer, and there were at least 30 bulbs in that drawer, all unpackaged. I grabbed one, climbed up the ladder (his ceilings were 10 feet high), unscrewed the old bulb, screwed the new one in, I climbed back down the ladder, and switched the switch. Nothing happened, I figured he must have blown a fuse.

I asked him where the fuse box was, he didn't understand, he just kept repeating, "lights out Jim." I looked in his basement, which was right off the kitchen, and found the fuse box. Everything looked OK, I checked the wiring going from the basement to the kitchen, it looked good. I took the plate off the switch, everything seemed to be in order.

I couldn't imagine what the problem might be, I grabbed another light bulb, back up the ladder, tried it, nothing, back down the ladder. Grab another bulb, and it's back up the ladder again, nothing. I had an idea, I will get a voltage tester. Back to my house up the street, grab a voltage tester, back to his house. Back up the ladder with the tester. Everything tested OK, he had power there, I decided to try one more bulb.

I handed him the old bulb and noticed that he put it back in the same drawer! He was saving all his old bulbs! I asked him if he had a good bulb, and he opened up a different drawer, and there they were, all packaged and ready to go. I screwed it in, and presto, "lights on!"

He had a dog named Trigger who was the meanest son of a bitch I had ever seen. He made Godzilla look like a fairy princess, and it seemed that he hated me. Rusty and I were standing on my front steps one afternoon, and up the street comes Trigger with John in hot pursuit yelling," get him Jim". He spotted me, and all hell broke loose. I made a mad dash for my side door, but alas, I was too late.

He was on me like a new suit, biting my ass as I ran, he must have got at least two good bites before I got to the door of the hallway, and even then, my getaway job was not finished. He took one last bite and latched on before I was halfway through the door.

Battling the dog, the pain, and now the door, my mother opened the door at the top of the steps and yelled down, "what are you doing to John's dog?" And I replied," he's fine mom." John finally got Trigger to let go, and he turned to me and said," thanks Jim" wincing I said, "sure John."

He had a huge tree branch rubbing the power lines to his house, and decided to cut it down. He walked up the street to Mr. Trunick's house to get a ladder, "Yo Yode, ya got a ladder?" Mr. Trunick told him he did have one, and he would send it down with Paul when he returned from the store.

When Paul returned home from the store, he said he would gladly take the ladder down to John's house. When he performed the task, he decided to stay and watch and offer his help if need be. John's brothers, Jim, Joe, and Bill were all there too, I guess to offer moral support, although, the three of them were "as useless as tits on a bull" (my father used to say).

John and Jim set the ladder up against the tree. John grabbed a saw & climbed the ladder, it couldn't have been any higher than 10 feet. He got to the top, shimmied himself out on the branch, and proceeded to saw off the branch he was sitting on!
His brother Bill, the stutterer, tried to tell him what he was doing, "h-h-hey J-J-J-John, l-l-lookit w-w-what y-y-your d-d-doing!" John said, "shut up you nut, I know what I'm doing." He kept sawing away. The best part about it was, the three brothers were standing directly beneath John, Paul mentioned to them that they should move, and they just shrugged him off.

John was pretty proud of himself, he was finally doing something right, or so he thought. A couple more passes with the saw and down it came John, branch and all.

He bowled over all three brothers with the one-shot, Paul told me it was a sight to see, all four on the ground at the same time. "They got up quickly," Paul said, "gathered their composure and went in the house".

"I don't suffer from insanity, I enjoy every minute of it!"

CHAPTER 28.

To Be Young Again

I hate to admit it, but my drinking days as a teenager included, but was not limited to: wines: Silver Satin, Bali Hai, Pluck, Thunderbird, Orange Extract, Lemon Extract, Almond Extract, Wild Irish Rose, Ripple. And every kind of beer known to man. You will notice, that I stuck the Extracts in there. We drank those because of their high alcohol content.

We would always end up getting sick, but we kept on drinking them anyway. They were a cheap high, and you didn't have to be 21 to buy them. I am totally amazed that neither Rusty, nor I, did not die of alcohol poisoning!

"IRS: We've got what it takes to take what you have got. "

CHAPTER 29.

Lady on the Hill

On a sad note, I recall one Sunday afternoon, Sparkle and I, were getting ready for church, and we heard a voice screaming, "help me, somebody please help me," coming from the Cemetery.

We looked out the attic window to see a woman coming down the hill screaming and crying at the same time. We watched her make her way down, stumbling and falling along the way. She finally fell and stayed there still crying. Sparkle told me to stay there and call the police, while she made her way up to the woman.

Sparkle approached her, and asked her if she was all right. Still in shock, she managed to tell Sparkle her story, her name was Rita Thompson, she was at the Italian Club the previous night, and met a man who offered to take her home. She accepted his offer and jumped in his car.

He took her to the Highwood Cemetery entrance, she froze, too scared to move anything but her mouth, she screamed, but it was too late at night for anybody to hear her.

He took her through the Cemetery and stopped there at the top of our hill and proceeded to attack her, beating her, tearing at her clothes, she fended him off managing to get the door open, running, screaming. She must have scared him however, he drove off, leaving her to scream and cry.

How do you decide who to marry?

"Time is the best teacher, unfortunately it kills all of its students !"

CHAPTER 30.

No Heat

On a lighter note, when I was 16 and in a" I can do anything" mode. I decided that I was going to learn how to wash and dry clothes. I stuck a load of clothes in the washing machine, no problem.

When that load was washed, I pulled the clothes from the washing machine, and threw them into the dryer, no problem. I waited till the little buzzer rang, and pulled the clothes out of the dryer, clothes were still wet, problem. I stuck them in again for another 15 minutes. The buzzer rang, and I pulled the clothes out again..., still wet. My decision was that the clothes dryer went on the fritz, and I thought to save my mother a $75 charge from a service repair man, I would repair it myself.

I called Collins Appliance, the local repair parts store, and explained to the counter man (his name was Ed) what the problem was, and he said it sounded like the ceramic glow coil, (the part that ignites the flame) was bad, and he explained to me, where the part was, and how to remove it. So I did what Ed told me to do, and took it to him. He brought the new one out to me and said, "you must be very careful clipping this back in, for it is ceramic and it will crack with one wrong move. The part cost $45, and it is very fragile."

"$45!" I exclaimed, "why so much?" He said, "supply and demand, the part very rarely goes bad, and the fact that it is ceramic, makes it hard to manufacture." I thanked Ed for his instructions, and took the part home to put it in. I was very careful snapping it into place, I turned the dryer back on, no heat. I called Ed backup and explained to him what happened. He said that the glow coil must be defective, to bring it down and he will replace it. I started to unclip it, but something went very wrong, it cracked in my hands, and came apart into pieces.

I took it to Ed, and he said, "I'm sorry, but you will have to pay the full price for another one, we can't take this back the way it is." So I paid him the $45 reluctantly, and took the part home.

I was very careful to put the part in, but I forgot to pull the plug on the dryer and got knocked on my ass putting it back in. It went in without any trouble, I turned the dryer on, still the clothes were not drying! I was very frustrated at this point, I was very careful to unclip it, but as I was putting it back in the box, I dropped it, and it broke into a million tiny pieces.

I went back to Ed to purchase another one, he asked me what happened, I told him, and he said he would tell his manager what was going on, and see if there was anything he could do.

He left me standing at the counter waiting. After a couple of minutes, Ed came back and said to me, "I'm sorry Jim, but my manager said there was nothing he could do, you will have to buy another one." I handed him a check for $45, fortunately my job at Keystone plumbing warranted me to do so (but it was *putting one hell of a dent in my account). I took the new part, and was on my way. I put in the new part in gently, said a prayer, and turned the dryer on, nothing!*

By now, I was suicidal, I called Ed back, "whatever could be the problem?" Ed said, "check your setting again, is it on heat?." I went to the dryer, and this is what it read; AIR DRY: NO HEAT!.

I switched the setting to heat, Bingo!

> *Only in America...do banks leave both doors open and then chain the pens to the counters!

CHAPTER 31.

My Family

The gang went their separate ways over the years. Paul went to Vietnam, Porjy and Rusty went into the service too. I was classified 1-Y which meant I would only be drafted in time of war, because of my lazy eye. I stayed on Smithton Street the longest until 1999. I am still a, registered master plumber with Allegheny County, forced into retirement by a disabling injury.

I grew up on the North Side of Pittsburgh Pennsylvania, got married at 20 years old in 1972 and have been married ever since, to a wonderful woman, Maggie (nicknamed Angel Cake). We have four awesome children, Carolynn, (we nicknamed her Carrie, or Fruitcake) she will be 30 October 3rd of this year(2005). Next comes the twins. Christopher, (nicknamed Cupcake) born first, just turned 27 on April 29th engaged to Jessica Lepore, Jeffery (nicknamed Beefcake) who also turned 27 married to Olivia Carroll well over a year ago. And last but not least, is our baby Craig (Nicknamed Crackers) who just turned 24 on March 25th. Just for the record, I am nicknamed Poundcake also.

And how could I forget, my one grandchild, Maranda (nicknamed Mandi, she's Pappap's Little Moppet ask her, she will tell you, and will be two years old in December this year.)

(Update: it's now 2010, and I'd like to fill you in on my growing family. Maggie and I are still together after 38 years, Carrie and Scott are still together, Maranda is seven years old. They've added a new little girl since the writing of this book; Trinity Ruth will be two in November. Chris and Jessica, have a 15-month-old boy; Elias James, Jeff and Liv have a bouncing baby girl; Delia Jean, who is 14 months. My baby Craig, found himself a dynamite woman by the name of Rachel Lucas (whom I call Sunshine), they got married last October, and presented us with a little eight week old boy by the name of Adrian Joseph. Thanks to modern technology, I am able to watch my grandchildren grow by means of a WebCam camera mounted on top of my monitor. So far, I've watched Delia, and Elias take their first steps!!!)

In 1999, after 27 years of marriage, living mostly in the same house, and thanks to a sizable settlement from a car accident that Maggie had. She and I decided to build our dream home, a log home. And as I said before, I am a registered master plumber, so naturally, I installed the plumbing and the radiant heat in the house. Everything was going along smoothly, Maggie works for a law firm as a bookkeeper. I would pick her up after work, take her home to get changed, we would both go the 20 miles to the new house, and work there most of the evening with spotlights, and a generator for lighting.

CHAPTER 32.

The Fall

There is no drywall in our home its all-tongue and groove cedar wood. We usually worked until midnight, we went home exhausted, only to go to bed and start the process over again. The whole thing was worth it, because it turned into a beautiful log home.

Moved in now, August 28, 2000, I was watching a football game after working a 16 hour day. During the game, I did partake a couple glasses of Chianti wine. The football game was over around 11:00 PM, and I wasn't tired, so, I stuck in a John Denver Wildlife Concert DVD and finished watching that. When that was over I got up, shut the TV off, turned out all the lights, and proceeded up the steps to the bedroom. We hadn't finished the steps yet, so there was no railing. Not realizing how tired I was, (or how stupid I was) climbing the steps in the dark, with no railing, can be hazardous to your health.

I walked right over the side of the steps, and fell 8 feet to the hardwood floor, breaking my neck in six places. Fortunately my dog, Nessie, saved my life that evening, I couldn't move, I tried screaming for Maggie, but all that came out of me was faint whispers. Nessie to the rescue, she ran around me, charged up the stairs to the bedroom, and started barking. She barked until Maggie woke up and wanted to find out what the problem was. Maggie came to the top of the steps, seen me lying there on the floor, and called the paramedics immediately.

They life flighted me to Allegheny General Hospital, it was there I lost a week, in and out of consciousness in trauma. I spent three long week's in intensive care, and then to rehab. I spent three grueling months in therapy. They got me walking with a walker, but I still could not use my hands.

I went to a neurosurgeon, he told me my spinal column was too narrow, that my spinal cord had no room, if he operated and decompressed the spinal column, I would have a better chance of getting my hands back. I opted to do that, and had the operation. I waited a year, and not only did it not help, I started to get sharp pains in my lower back and terrible spasms. I was in a lot of pain, and did not know which way to turn.

Someone told me about a system called a baclofen pump installed in your abdomen and it distributes baclofen (a medicine to control spasms) directly to your spine. Again, I opted to go with the operation. It helped with the spasms,.

But it did not help the pain. I had heard somewhere that morphine could be added to the pump to ease the pain. I opted to have that done. It eased the pain for a short while, but then after that, it came back, hitting me like a freight train, every time I tried to take a step.

The therapy on my hands, was not working, the more I tried to work them, the tighter they became. It got to the point in therapy, that I just wasn't getting anywhere. It seems that God has a different plan for me. I had to eventually stop going to therapy because of the nonproductiveness. All the while, the state, (Occupational Vocational Rehabilitation) did a lot of funding for my rehabilitation. They bought me some neat stuff to help me start a business

1.) A new computer, printer, and scanner

2.) Video-editing equipment (over $3000 worth) and for exercising at home, a new treadmill. What they didn't supply me with, is somebody to teach me how to edit films. So I made up my own my own business.

3.) A standing frame, to help me stand, and

4.) A Hoyer lift, to help pick me up when I do something stupid, like falling on my ass!

"How Can I Miss You if You Won't Go Away?"

CHAPTER 33.

My New Business

I called a handful of contractors, (I personally knew a good bit of them, I was in the plumbing trade for 30 years) and asked them if they would like to try to engage in the referral business with me. They asked me what it was all about, I explained to them: I advertise as a handyman (plumber's, heating contractors, painters, electricians, and etc.) and when the people call me, I hook them up with the contractor, for 20% of their profit. I started in January of this year, and haven't showed a profit yet but it takes time. I also, above all things, write children's stories!

Only in America...do we order a double cheeseburger, large fries, and a diet coke!

CAST OF CHARACTERS

(And I Do Mean Characters!)

In March of this year (2005) I made a phone call to all the guys, to see if they wanted to get together to play poker once a month. Porjy, Rusty, Tony, Tank, Chuck, Don, and Rich all agreed to it and that's what we do, we play poker the third Friday of every month! Most of us have jobs and here is what we do:

Me, Jim Ehrhardt = I run a referral service, I hook-up clients with contractors for a minimal service fee, I also write stories.

Paul Trunick—retired from State Penitentiary as prison guard, moved to Florida

Rusty Waxler—superintendent for a local Manufacturing plant, making buffers.

Chuck Wooster—owns his own business, importing & exporting linens

Porjy (Nut) Retterback—retired, works for his son-in-laws contracting business.

Don (Sctultz) Retterback—works as a project manager in the field for a local contracting firm.

Rich Masik-. Deceased

Tank Arlet—works as an engineer for a local engineering firm.

Tim Arlet—works maintenance at a local University, and has a contracting business.

Linda (Ehrhardt) Shelleby-retired, worked as a secretary for a local school

Tony (Nino) Tusa—works as a guidance counselor for the mentally challenged

Jimmy Long—Deceased

THE END